JOSÉ ALTUVE

Champion Baseball Star

David Aretha

Enslow Publishing
101 W. 23rd Street
Suite 240
New York, NY 10011
USA
enslow.com

Published in 2018 by Enslow Publishing, LLC.

101 W. 23rd Street, Suite 240, New York, NY 10011

Library of Congress Cataloging-in-Publication Data

Names: Aretha, David, author.
Title: José Altuve : Champion Baseball Star / David Aretha.
Description: New York : Enslow Publishing, 2018. | Series: Sports Star
  Champions | Includes bibliographical references and index. | Audience:
  Grade 6-8.
Identifiers: LCCN 2017003410| ISBN 9780766086906 (library-bound) | ISBN
  9780766087491 (pbk.) | ISBN 9780766087507 (6-pack)
Subjects: LCSH: Altuve, José, 1990-–Juvenile literature. | Baseball
  players—Venezuela—Biography—Juvenile literature. | Baseball
  players—United States—Biography—Juvenile literature.
Classification: LCC GV865.A65 A74 2018 | DDC 796.357092 [B] —dc23
LC record available at https://lccn.loc.gov/2017003410

Printed in the United States of America

To Our Readers: We have done our best to make sure all websites in this book were active and appropriate when we went to press. However, the author and the publisher have no control over and assume no liability for the material available on those websites or on any websites they may link to. Any comments or suggestions can be sent by email to customerservice@enslow.com.

Photo Credits: Cover, p. 1 Justin Berl/Getty Images; pp. 4, 10 Icon Sports Wire/Getty Images; pp. 6, 25, 30 © AP Images; p. 9 ekler/Shutterstock.com; p. 11 karengesweinphotography/Shutterstock.com; p. 16 Thomas B. Shea/Getty Images; pp. 18, 32, 34, 39 Bob Levey/Getty Images; p. 20 Eric Christian Smith/Getty Images; pp. 23, 28 Stacy Revere/Getty Images; p. 26 Matt Brown/Getty Images; p. 33 Josh Haunschild/Major League Baseball/Getty Images; p. 37 Mark Cunningham/Getty Images; p. 40 Elsa/Getty Images; p. 43 Scott Halleran/Getty Images.

Contents

Altuve's explosive quickness and surprising strength blast the ball over 400 feet (121 m). In 2016, he socked twenty-four pitches out of the park.

Introduction:
Falling Just Short

José Altuve badly wanted to hit for the cycle, but he fell just short. Literally, he *fell* just short.

It was June 25, 2016, and the Houston Astros were visiting the Kansas City Royals, the reigning World Series champions. As the evening game began, players sweated in 93°F (33°C) heat. Altuve (pronounced *al TOO vay*) embraced the hot weather. He had grown up in Maracay, Venezuela, where the average daytime high in February was 90°F (32°C). He had also played his entire six-year Major League career with Houston, a steam bath all summer long.

Altuve entered the game red-hot. He was batting .340, one point short of his American League (AL) best average of .341 in 2014. He normally batted leadoff for the Astros, which made sense. After all, he had led the American League in stolen bases in both 2014 (56) and 2015 (38). But in 2016, he often batted in the third spot in the lineup to take advantage of his emerging power. Altuve had already belted twelve home runs during the 2016 season. Launching balls out into the seats is an impressive accomplishment for any baseball player, but especially for José. After all, he was only 5 foot 5 (165 centimeters). He was the shortest player in the Major Leagues since shortstop Freddie Patek, who had debuted in the majors in 1968.

Altuve smiles after tripping over second base, in his failed effort to hit for the cycle, on June 25, 2016.

On this night, Altuve continued to flash his power stroke. In the first inning, he blasted a double to deep center field. In the third, he rocketed an enormous home run to left field—his second 440-foot (134-m) bomb in six days. And he didn't let up. In the fourth, he punched a single to right field. He now had a single, double, and home run, meaning he needed just a triple to complete "the cycle"—a rare feat that every hitter covets.

In the sixth inning, Altuve had his chance. He drilled a pitch to the wall in left-center, and his eyes flashed like a locomotive's as he motored around first base. As he dug toward second—craving that triple—his helmet flew off. And then, as he tried to cut the corner hard at second, he crashed and burned. He had run so hard that he stumbled and fell face-first.

As Altuve lay in the dirt, after settling for a double, he looked toward the Astros dugout. Teammate George Springer and his other buddies were rolling with laughter. Altuve, too, beamed a big grin and chuckled. "Everybody got a good laugh out of it," said manager A. J. Hinch.

Besides his spectacular skills, the little man has a wonderful sense of humor. He's full of enthusiasm and flashes a million-dollar smile. After the game, Altuve had no trouble making fun of himself. "I've seen it already on social media," he said. "'Altuve blew a tire.'"

Four days later in Los Angeles, Altuve was back at it, trying mightily to hit for the cycle again. He singled in the first, tripled in the third, and doubled in the fifth against the Angels. He didn't clear the fences, but his lineout in the sixth and sharp single in the ninth had fans shaking their heads in amazement. He ended the day—Houston's last game of the month—with a .357 average. He had batted .420 in June.

In the stands that afternoon, visiting Astros fans chanted, "MVP! MVP! MVP!" The chant echoed the thoughts of many baseball experts. This stunningly small second baseman—this five-foot-five package of dynamite—could possibly be the best baseball player in the world.

"I'll Sign for Free"

José Altuve loved baseball so much that he was willing to sign with the Houston Astros for free.

The year was 2006. In his native country of Venezuela, a poor nation on the northern tip of South America, José attended a tryout camp. The Astros were looking for talented players from a country that had produced such stars as slugger Miguel Cabrera and pitcher Felix Hernandez. At the time José was just sixteen years old. He could rip line drives with his quick swing, and he could run like a blaze of glory. However, his defense at second base was subpar, and he was short and skinny.

After the workout, José was told that he wasn't good enough to play professional baseball. At that moment, he could have given up and gone home. Instead, he came back to the field the next day.

"I knew in my heart I was good enough to make it," Altuve said. "I told them I wanted another chance."

Al Pedrique gave him that chance. A former Major League manager, he now scouted for the Astros. Pedrique liked José's electrifying swing and was impressed by the kid's parents. "Very respectful family, very polite," Pedrique said. "And he's the same way. So it got my attention, the way he handled himself."

José grew up in the industrial city of Maracay, Venezuela. Detroit Tigers superstar Miguel Cabrera also hails from Maracay.

Critics thought José was too short to play in the majors, but Astros scout Al Pedrique believed in him.

Soon, Omar Lopez of the Astros approached Altuve. Lopez recalled the conversation.

"We would like to give you a contract and have the chance to play for the Astros," Lopez told José.

"Really, Omar, really?" José replied.

"Yeah. We would like to talk to your father, your mother to see what you're looking for, you know, signing bonus-wise."

"Signing bonus? Just give me a contract. I'll sign for free."

In pro baseball, quality players don't sign for free. In 2006, dozens of amateur players earned signing bonuses of over $1 million.

Pedrique wanted to give Altuve a $20,000 signing bonus, but a colleague said, no, he's too short. So the bonus became $15,000. It was the greatest investment the Astros ever made.

José inherited his love of baseball from his father, Carlos Altuve. In fact, while his mother, Lastenia, was giving birth to José on May 6, 1990, Carlos was at a nearby ballpark. He knew the birth was imminent, but he was glued to the action on the field. "They ran from the hospital to the stadium to tell my dad, 'Hey, you have your kid already!'" José said. "He said, 'Okay, okay, let's go!' He was a big fan of baseball."

José enjoyed a happy childhood in Maracay, Venezuela. Known as the "Garden City," Maracay was a densely populated city of nearly a million people. His father worked as an assistant to engineers at a chemical company, and his mother stayed home with her two boys—José and younger brother Carlos. One day, she said, "Santa Claus brought [José] a bat, ball, and glove. And every day he would wait religiously for his dad with his little bat and ball."

When José was a young child, he received the best Christmas gifts ever: a bat, a baseball, and a glove.

There's No Crying in Baseball

One day during his first Minor League season, José called home. He had mustered just two hits in his last thirty at-bats, he said, almost crying. "You have two options," his dad advised. "Man up and start hitting, or tell the team to buy you a plane ticket and come home—if you're going to cry every time things go wrong." "That was the only time," his father said. "He understood the message."

Beginning when José was four, Carlos came home from work and played ball at the field with José. "He was in love with the sport," his dad said, "and that is why he is driven."

In a documentary for MLB Network, José and his father returned to the ball field. The humble field was uneven and dusty with patches of grass. "Sometimes we just had one ball," José said. "He'd throw it to me, I'd hit it, and he went back to pick the ball up and come back here."

He said the worst part was when he'd hit a foul ball onto the roof of a nearby building. "We'd have to go back to the house and start planning. How are we gonna get a ball? Sometimes getting a ball [was] not that easy."

José recalled the first baseball game he ever played. "I was seven years old and I just loved it," he said. "It was so much fun. I knew right then that baseball is what I wanted to do, that I wanted to go to the United States and play in the big leagues when I grew up."

"Growing up" would be an issue for Altuve. After signing with the Astros in 2006, he barely grew in height. Years later, he still looked like a youngster. One day, he recalled, he showed up at the ballpark in Maracay to play a Winter League game. "The security guard wouldn't let me in," José said. "He told me, 'You're not a player. I got a son the same size as you—and he's eight years old.'"

José maintained a sense of humor about his height, but he took his game extremely seriously. As a seventeen-year-old in the Venezuelan Summer League in 2007, he batted .343—sixth in the league. A year later, he moved to the United States and debuted in the Minor Leagues. From 2008 to 2010, he played for Greeneville, Tri-City, and Lexington. He always hit around .300 while stealing bases and improving his defense at second base.

> **"A couple people [thought] he was cocky, a hot dog. I said, 'No, he's not a hot dog—that's the way he is. He loves to play the game, he enjoys it, and he has a lot of confidence.'"**
> —Astros scout Al Pedrique

In 2011, Altuve took his game to a higher level. He smashed .408 in fifty-two games for Class-A Lancaster, then cracked .361 in thirty-five games for Double-A Corpus Christi. On July 19, he was leading the Minor Leagues with a .389 batting average. The Astros had seen enough. That day, they traded their starting second baseman, Jeff Keppinger, and promoted Altuve to the big leagues. Yet the question remained: Was he too small to handle Major League pitching?

"Everybody is going to see José and see his stature and begin to question his ability," said Astros General Manager Ed Wade. "In that case, people are really going to underestimate what this kid is all about. He's got a chance to be a really good big-league player."

Though just twenty-one years old, Altuve wouldn't need time to develop. With Houston, he was about to become an overnight sensation.

2

A New Sensation

Sure, rookie José Altuve was batting .314, but at least San Francisco Giants pitcher Madison Bumgarner didn't have to worry about him hitting a home run. It was August 20, 2011, and José had yet to homer in his twenty-eight MLB games. And besides, the little guy was a foot shorter than the 6-foot-5 (195-cm) pitcher.

At Houston's Minute Maid Park, Altuve unloaded on a Bumgarner pitch and drove it 400 feet (121 m) to center field. No, it didn't clear the fence, but it flew over outfielder Cody Ross's head. As he rounded second, Altuve turned on the jets. "Altuve's gonna sprint toward third," blared Astros announcer Bill Brown. "He'll make it easily." Third base coach Dave Clark put up his hands, signaling for Altuve to stop with a triple. But the rookie didn't let up. "He's going to run through the stop sign!" Raymond screamed. "And score!" Altuve had used his power *and* speed to produce an inside-the-park home run.

"I just kept running hard...," Altuve said. "When I realized there was a sign, it was too late."

All season long, Altuve kept on hitting. He rapped .276 as a rookie, then cracked .339 in the Venezuelan Winter League (VWL). Between the minors, the majors, and the VWL, he amassed a staggering 282 hits on the year.

Altuve motors around third base during his inside-the-park home run on August 20, 2011.

> "Everywhere I go, I have to prove myself. I have to go a little harder than everybody else."
>
> —José Altuve

The Astros finished 56–106 in 2011, the worst season in the team's fifty-year history. A year later they went 55–107. Houston's offense was so bad that J.D. Martinez led the club with just 55 RBI. Meanwhile, General Manager Jeff Luhnow tried to remain positive. "Look at José Altuve," he said. "He's a great story. He'll always be an underdog because of his size. But if he has success, people will be saying they know who plays second base for the Houston Astros, as opposed to, 'Who are those guys?'"

Altuve certainly sparked excitement. In 2012, he batted .360 through May 4, and on June 10 against the Chicago White Sox he homered and stole home. The twenty-two-year-old represented the Astros at the MLB All-Star Game, earning a major feature story in *USA Today*. "Altuve exudes neither a Napoleon complex nor shyness, but rather behaves like someone comfortable with himself," stated the article's author, José L. Ortiz. "He shows a sense of humor about his stature, such as when he jumped to meet teammates' ultra-high-fives following a home run earlier this season, but makes it clear he's ready to compete."

Altuve finished the 2012 season with a .290 average, thirty-three steals, and eighty runs, earning MVP honors. He also belted seven homers with his quick, explosive swing. "Don't take him easy because he'll definitely take you hard," said Washington pitcher Gio Gonzalez. "He swings hard and he makes sure to let you know, 'Hey, I'm no joke.'"

The Astros sought a fresh start in 2013 when they moved from the National League Central to the American League West. (The move balanced out the number of teams in each league, from 16/14 to 15/15.) To celebrate, the Astros brought back their old mascot from the 1990s, Orbit. But the green, alien-faced creature brought no luck. The Astros went 51–111—one of the worst records in Major League history. Jordan Lyles led the pitching staff in victories with just seven.

José doesn't mind leaping for high-fives. His energy sparks the Astros' offense, and he always wants to play. In 2016, he missed only one game.

José versus Goliath

On May 1, 2012, Altuve faced New York Mets reliever Jon Rauch. At 6-foot-11 (210 cm), Rauch was the tallest player ever in the Major Leagues. "Altuve walked up to home plate," joked Astros announcer Jim Deshaies, "and said, 'I will smite thee!'" Altuve lined out to the first baseman. The 18-inch (45-cm) difference between Rauch and José was the greatest in MLB history—with one exception. On August 19, 1951, in a publicity stunt, 3-foot-7 (109-cm) Eddie Gaedel batted for the St. Louis Browns against the Detroit Tigers. "Keep it low," catcher Bob Swift told pitcher Bob Cain. Gaedel walked on four pitches.

Once again, Altuve started strong in 2013, ripping .342 through May 18, and once again, he wilted as the summer went on. Perhaps it was because of the relentless heat in Houston, but those who thought the little guy couldn't handle the rigors of a full season were wrong. He bounced back with a .357 average in the month of September—tops in the American League. He finished the year batting .283 with 35 stolen bases.

Along the way, Altuve developed into a superb fielder at second base. Though he didn't possess the strongest arm or greatest range, he led AL second basemen in turning double plays (114) in 2013. His .987 fielding percentage ranked fifth in the league at his position. "That's something that

I'm really working on," Altuve said in late May. "I've been putting 100 percent of work into defense like I do hitting because that way I can help my team more. I feel like I'm getting a lot better."

In 2014, the Astros improved to a competitive 70–92. Chris Carter belted 37 home runs, and lefty Dallas Keuchel (12–9, 2.93 ERA) starred on the mound. But the big story was Altuve's historic production. He led the AL in batting (.341), becoming Houston's first-ever batting champion and the

In 2013 and 2014, Altuve led AL second basemen in double plays turned. In 2015, he won his first Gold Glove Award.

Majors' shortest hitting champ since 5-foot-4 (162-cm) Wee Willie Keeler in 1898. Not only did Altuve lead the AL in hits (225) and steals (56), but he became the first MLB player to amass 225 hits, 56 steals, and 47 doubles since Ty Cobb in 1911. After he stole two bases in four consecutive games, the Baseball Hall of Fame called. They wanted his cleats.

With his lightning-quick stroke, José was ripping everything in the strike zone—and sometimes out of it. His ability to hammer every pitch in sight frustrated Kansas City catcher Salvador Perez. "He's one of those guys I don't know where to put it for the pitcher," Perez said. "I don't know what to call."

Against lefties in 2014, Altuve smashed .414. He had such command of the strike zone that he struck out only 7.5 percent of the time, the second-best mark in the Majors. In ten games, he batted fourth in the lineup, cleanup, a spot normally reserved for a team's best power hitter. Altuve played in the All-Star Game and won a Silver Slugger Award as the best-hitting second baseman in the league. In AL MVP Award voting, he finished thirteenth, indicating he was one of the game's greatest players.

"That's one of the cool things about baseball," said Hunter Pence, Altuve's former teammate. "Tall, small, we all have different ways of getting it done. He's been spectacular, and it's pretty amazing to watch."

How Does He Do It?

José's fifty-eight-point improvement in batting average from 2013 to 2014 (.283 to .341) didn't happen by accident. Something didn't just "click"; he didn't suddenly just "get hot." No, he worked for every extra point of that average.

Unhappy with his hitting in 2013, José bore down in the winter months and into the next season. He focused more on his nutrition and training, becoming leaner and stronger. He already had phenomenal hand-eye coordination and a super-quick swing, but he found ways to improve at the plate. He spent countless hours studying opposing pitchers on video, concocting a plan of attack against each opponent. Prior to games, he expanded on normal pregame batting practice

Through thousands of hours of practice, José has developed a near-flawless swing. From 2014 to 2016, he led the AL in hits every year.

with indoor batting practice and more video study. If something was a bit off in his swing, he worked to iron out the kinks. His goal: perfect batting mechanics.

"The way he thinks through at-bats…the way he has a plan for what he's trying to do, he's very elite at his preparation," said A. J. Hinch, who became Houston's new manager in September 2014.

Pitchers succeed by firing pitches to perfect spots; for example, a slider just off the outside corner. But Altuve foils them by drilling even the perfect pitches. "He can do anything with the bat," Hinch said. "He can handle sliders, he can handle fastballs."

He can even handle pitches over his head. On September 22, 2014, against Texas, he jumped to swing at a pitch that was about 6 feet (1.8 meters) above the plate, fouling it off. "That was a hit-and-run," he explained. "You have to put the ball in play or at least protect the runner, so that's what I did."

"He's tough to explain, other than the fact he works as hard or harder than anyone, he's got freakish hand-eye skills, he loves baseball, and he wants to be great."

—David Stearns, the Astros' assistant general manager

Altuve's workout routines are becoming legendary. In spring training in 2015, he told ESPN.com that he arrived at the ballpark every day no later than 6:30 a.m.—while most players were still curled up in bed. And in April 2015, the documentary *Big Dreams: The José Altuve Story* revealed his startling offseason workouts in Venezuela. Working with personal trainer Felix Pacheco, José would pull a large and heavy tire along the pavement, jump *over* the tall tire, and bash the tire repeatedly with a sledgehammer. "Tighten your abs," Pacheco ordered as José pounded the rubber as if it were a fastball. "Six, seven, eight—breathe."

José warms up during spring training in 2015. After a winter of grueling workouts, he was in tiptop shape.

Thunder and Lightning

Given his size, fans might expect that Altuve's home runs barely clear the outfield fences. Not true. According to ESPN's Home Run Tracker, José's twenty-four homers in 2016 averaged a whopping 399 feet (121 m). Incredibly, he launched four of his bombs over 440 feet (134 m), including a 448-foot (136-m) smash at Baltimore. Of course, José provides "lightning" as well as "thunder." During a triple that he legged out at Arizona in 2015, MLB's Statcast measured his top speed at 20.9 miles per hour (33 kmh). He is also one of a few players who could reach first base on a ground ball in under 4.0 seconds.

José averaged 38 stolen bases per season from 2012 to 2016. In June 2014, he became the first MLB player in ninety-seven years to record four straight multi-steals games.

"The most important thing about José is his drive," Pacheco said. "He's tireless."

Altuve's increasing strength resulted in greater power—from seven homers in 2014 to fifteen in 2015 to an eye-popping twenty-four in 2016. Including José, only ten men 5-foot-5 (165 cm) or shorter have played in the Major Leagues. Six of them never hit a home run in the majors. None of the other three—Wee Willie Keeler, Rabbit Maranville, and Freddie Patek—ever hit more than six homers in a season. Nor did they ever build their muscles with a tire and sledgehammer.

In recent years, José has learned to lay off bad pitches. He used to swing at deliveries that were a couple inches outside the strike zone, drilling many of them for hits. However, hurlers exploited his aggressiveness by throwing even farther out of the zone, hoping he would chase. Now that he tries to swing at only strikes, pitchers have to keep the ball closer to the edges. That means José gets better pitches to hit.

For José, being short actually comes with some advantages. Defensively, it's easier for a diminutive second baseman to stay low on ground balls. That way, the ball is more at eye level when it comes at him. At the plate, he has a smaller strike zone top to bottom than any other player. Pitchers thus have a harder

Being short allows Altuve to stay low on grounders, which helps him to see the ball into his glove. Through 2016, his .988 career fielding percentage ranked twenty-second all-time among MLB second basemen.

time throwing him strikes. Also, José's short arms actually benefit him at the plate. He's able to make a quick, direct slash at the ball, something very tall hitters can't do.

Altuve says that baseball scouts should not dismiss smaller players. "I think most of the people like the kind of player like Derek Jeter and Alex Rodriguez," Altuve said. "They're pretty tall and they can do everything. But as a scout, you have to give credit to a little guy too. See what they have. Who knows? See what they can bring to the table."

Making Dreams Come True

At Minute Maid Park on May 5, 2016, Altuve met a courageous fan. Dylan, in a wheelchair with glove and baseball cap, was battling terminal cancer. The two chatted for a while, and then Dylan said, "Okay, now you're going to hit a homer."

Altuve could have promised the boy a home run, but he didn't want to disappoint him.

"I was like, 'Eh, I hit a homer yesterday, so don't expect me to hit a homer today. I don't want to make you feel bad if I don't.'"

Altuve completes his home run trot in the first inning on May 5, 2016. His courageous pal Dylan had predicted it.

"He was like, 'Yes, you're going to make it. You will see.'"

Altuve led off the bottom of the first inning against Seattle, and on the third pitch his blast to left field flew 425 feet (129 m)—one of the longest home runs he had ever hit.

"As soon as I hit the home run and I got to second base, I remembered what he said," Altuve recalled in a quiet voice after the game. "I really like the kid. He was really happy to be here."

José continued to thrill Dylan throughout the game, adding two singles and a double.

"I hope God blesses him for what he's been through right now," Altuve said.

Throughout his career, José has exceeded expectations—and not just on the field. A. J. Hinch, who became Houston's new manager late in 2014, immediately became a fan of Altuve. "He's the epitome of everything that's right around the Astros," Hinch said in 2016. "He's a great example. He's a hard worker. He will play selflessly and never take any of the credit and will want all the blame."

"I used to watch guys who were shorter than me and use them as an inspiration ... [Now] I have little guys tell me, 'Oh, if you can make it, I can make it."

—José Altuve

Unlike many foreign players, Altuve learned to speak fluent English early in his professional career. And while he is not yet an eloquent speaker in his second language, he always comes across as warm, humble, and sincere. In addition, he might have the brightest, cheeriest smile in all of baseball.

"He's an emotional guy, a passionate guy about pretty much every aspect of his life," said former Astros manager Bo Porter.

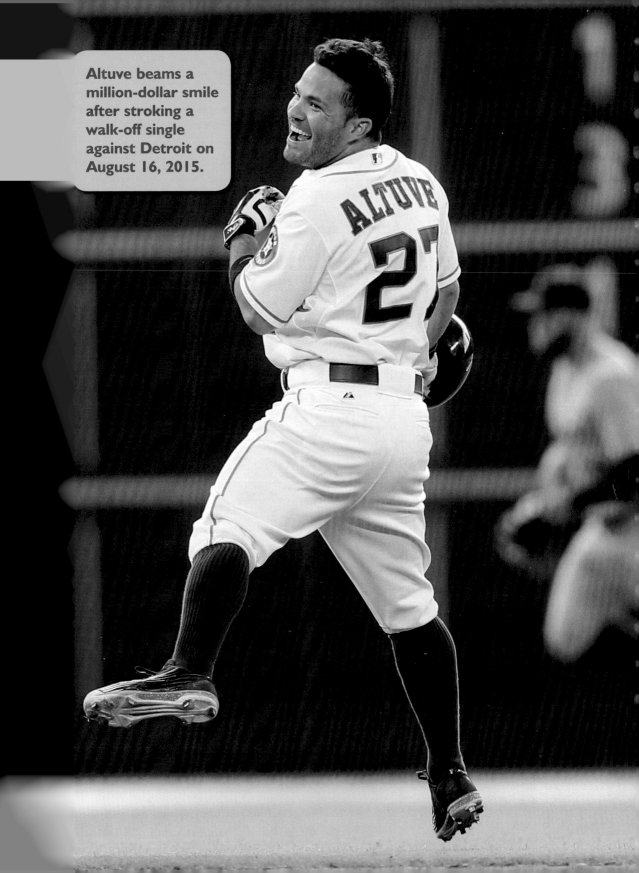

Altuve beams a million-dollar smile after stroking a walk-off single against Detroit on August 16, 2015.

How Many Altuves?

In 2012, Bryan Trostel of Houston debuted the website HowManyAltuves.com. The site uses an "Altuve" (five feet, five inches) as a unit of measurement. So, for example, if a bench is 10 feet, 10 inches long, it's 2.0 Altuves. Pretty soon, many people picked up on the craze. "How long is Palo Duro Canyon?" asked *Texas Monthly*. "116,965 Altuves." José embraced the new fad. When he appeared at the MLB Fan Cave, José and the two hosts measured things with a life-size cutout of him. They discovered that their giant TV was 3.25 Altuves wide, their hot dog was 0.09 Altuves, and that José himself was 1.0 Altuves—obviously.

José poses with his life-size cutout at the MLB Fan Cave in New York City. The Fan Cave guys measured their pool table's length at 1.5 Altuves.

In May 2013, José faced a difficult decision. His grandmother, whom he was very close to, died in Venezuela. He was torn between playing the next game and going home for the funeral. "I said, 'No, you're going home,'" Porter said. "Because even if you were to stay here, your mind, your heart, your soul would be back there with your family."

In 2016, José and his wife, Giannina, started a family of their own. On November 1, Giannina gave birth to a girl they named Melanie. In newborn pictures, Melanie was already smiling.

José has brought joy to many kids in Houston. In 2013, he was nominated for MLB's Roberto Clemente Award, which honors players who help the less fortunate. "His positive outlook, generous spirit, and commitment to excellence make him an ideal candidate for this prestigious award," said Astros General Manager Jeff Luhnow.

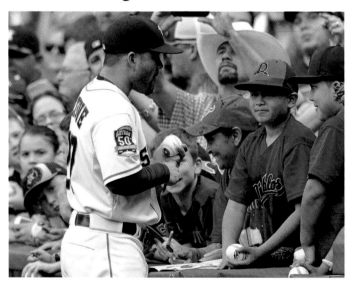

Starry-eyed kids ask for José's autograph at Houston's Minute Maid Park in August 2016. His autograph is now valued at around $130.

That year, Altuve supported two causes that helped at-risk kids in Houston. At new Community Leader park openings, Altuve personally congratulated hundreds of at-risk youth baseball and softball players for sticking with their studies and continuing to make healthy choices. He also taught baseball to kids at the Astros Urban Youth Academy, offering encouragement to those who were struggling on and off the field.

Also that year, he participated in the "Dancing with the 'Stros" charitable event, where he showed off his rhythm. He began the merengue by tossing his sparkly hat across the stage, then tore up the dance floor with partner Julie Rodriguez.

Despite all his success, José never forgets his hometown. Each offseason, he returns to Maracay, Venezuela, where "I wake up early every day and try to do something with my family," he said. His "family" includes aunts, uncles, and cousins as well as his longtime friends.

On Maracay's dusty ball fields, he swells with emotion when he sees poor, young kids with big-league dreams. "I come to my family every day and say, 'The little kids, what do they need? Do they need shoes to play? They need bats to play? Okay, I'll find them for you.'"

Those young ballplayers, particularly the smallest ones, look up to their hero and share the same thought: If José can achieve his dreams, I can too.

Player of the Year

Not even a bucket of water could cool off Altuve. On April 30, 2015, José was on fire. He ripped three hits that evening against the visiting Seattle Mariners, including a walk-off scorcher in the tenth inning. He upped his average to .367, and the 3–2 win gave Houston its eighth straight victory. Teammate George Springer celebrated by dousing José with a bucket of water. Two days later, Altuve belted a three-run homer on José Altuve Bobblehead Day at Minute Maid Park. The next day, the Astros won their tenth straight game, improving their record to 18–7.

All of a sudden, Houston was baseball's hottest team with an abundance of fresh, young talent. Bushy-bearded pitcher

Dallas Keuchel went 20–8, including 15–0 at home, and won the AL Cy Young Award. Five players clubbed over twenty home runs, including spectacular shortstop Carlos Correa. The five-tool twenty-year-old didn't join the team until June 8, but he won the AL Rookie of the Year Award with electrifying hitting and jaw-dropping defense.

In 2015, fans voted Altuve to the starting lineup in the MLB All-Star Game, making him the first Astros starter in seven years. José stood out in Cincinnati that night with a fluorescent long-sleeve shirt under his jersey and vibrant cleats in "ketchup" red and "mustard" yellow. That week, the Astros signed Altuve to a four-year contract extension. "José has quickly become the face of the franchise in less than two years, and we are excited to keep him here for many years to come," stated General Manager Jeff Luhnow.

Wearing his bright-colored cleats, Altuve batted eighth in the 2015 MLB All-Star Game. A year later, he was inserted as the leadoff batter—an indication of the respect he had gained.

Bobble Counter

On May 2, 2015, the Astros gave away José Altuve bobbleheads to the first ten thousand fans at the Saturday evening game against Seattle. But this was no ordinary bobblehead. It came with a hit counter, so that fans could keep track of every base hit that José ripped that season. Altuve had set an Astros record with 225 hits in 2014, and he would lead the American League with 200 knocks in 2015. He recorded only one hit in that May 2 game, but it was a big one: a three-run homer.

José didn't let up after the All-Star break. He played every game in August and reached base in each one of them. On the year, he ripped .313 while becoming the only Major Leaguer to amass 40 doubles, 15 homers, and 35 stolen bases. He became just the second American Leaguer ever to lead the league in hits (200) and steals (38) for a second consecutive season. As in 2014, he led the majors in batting against left-handers (.372).

After closing the season with fifty-one consecutive errorless games, Altuve led AL second basemen in fielding percentage at .993. He won his first AL Gold Glove Award, presented to the best defensive player at each position. He also received the first-ever Always Game Award, as voted

In April 2016, Altuve displayed the Silver Slugger Award and Gold Glove Award he had earned the previous season.

on by Major League players. The award is "given to the player who—game in and game out—constantly exhibits grit, tenacity, perseverance, and hustle; all for the benefit of his teammates and fans."

"Something you have to do every day is go out there and play hard for your team," he said when asked about the award. "Not for you—for your team, for the fans that come to the field and watch you play."

Altuve and outfielder Colby Rasmus celebrate Houston's victory over the Yankees in the 2015 AL Wild Card Game. José stole a base and drove in a run in the 3–0 victory.

After their hot start in 2015, the Astros cooled down. They finished with an 86–76 record and snuck into the playoffs. In the AL Wild Card Game, Keuchel and the bullpen shut out New York 3–0 at Yankee Stadium. Altuve knocked in the second run with a single in the seventh.

In the AL Division Series against the Kansas City Royals, José smashed three singles in the first five innings of Game 1. He scored in the first inning and drove in a run in the second to spark a 5–2 Astros win. Over the rest of the series, however, José went hitless in nineteen at-bats. The Astros could have clinched the series in Game 4, as they led 6–2 in the seventh, but the Royals rallied to win 9–6. KC breezed 7–2 in Game 5 to advance. "I got a lot of heartbroken guys in that clubhouse," Houston manager A. J. Hinch said afterward.

Altuve was among them, but the following spring he and his teammates returned with high hopes. In spring training 2016, MLB Network ranked José and Correa as the twelfth and thirteenth best players in baseball, and they soon proved worthy of the lofty praise. Altuve crushed five home runs in nine games in mid-April, and in June he batted a phenomenal .420. He was named the AL Player of the Month for June, a month in which Houston went 18–8 to improve to 42–37.

José once again started in the All-Star Game, and he continued to light up opposing pitchers. As late as August 20 he was batting .366. How remarkable is that? Ty Cobb has the highest career average in MLB history: .366. On September 1, CBSSports.com ranked José the number two player in the majors, behind Mike Trout. "Altuve continues on as perhaps the most complete player in baseball," the site proclaimed. "He hits for power, runs the bases exceptionally well, doesn't strike out, and mans a key defensive position. Consider him perhaps the favorite for AL MVP honors."

Astros fans agreed, often chanting "MVP! MVP!" when he stepped to the plate. On August 29, seven out of ten experts polled by *USA Today* said José was the league's most valuable player.

The Astros battled hard for a Wild Card spot but fell five wins short. Usually only players who make the playoffs earn league MVP awards, but on November 7 José was named one of three finalists for the top AL honor. His achievements were extraordinary. Altuve won his second batting title (.338) and led the league in hits (216) for the third year in a row. He amassed 24 home runs, 30 stolen bases, and 42 doubles, becoming only the fourth player in AL history to reach all of those totals in the same year. He also set career highs with 96 RBI (the same total that Correa had), 108 runs, 60 walks, a .396 on-base percentage, and a .531 slugging average. His .376 average on the road was the highest in the majors in twelve years.

> **"He just somehow, some way, hits it where the [defense] is not. I just think he can actually put the ball where he wants to."**
> —Astros outfielder George Springer on Altuve

On November 17, Major League Baseball announced that outfielder Mike Trout of the Los Angeles Angels of Anaheim had won the AL MVP Award. Outfielder Mookie Betts of Boston finished second, and Altuve placed third. Some blamed José's failure to win the award on his and Houston's mediocre finish. He batted .276 in September, and the Astros went 12–15 during the month.

Even when José asks the umpire for a time-out, he does so with a smile!

Nevertheless, José won an even more impressive award. The MLB Players' Association voted him the Major League Player of the Year. "Your *peers* think you're the best player in baseball," MLB Network's Greg Amsinger said to José. "Your thoughts." "It's an honor for me to be voted by the players," he said. "I appreciate it. I want to keep going like that and keep proving that we can play—and keep working hard."

That meant another offseason of grueling workouts—including, perhaps, more sledgehammer blows to the giant tire. Fans knew José would return in 2017 in peak condition, ready to wield more magic with his golden glove, fleet feet, and booming bat. And to think, he was still just twenty-six years old.

Stats, Honors, and Records

Year	TEAM	G	AB	R	H	2B	3B	HR	RBI	SB	BB	BA	OBP	SLG
\multicolumn{15}{c}{**JOSÉ ALTUVE'S MAJOR LEAGUE STATISTICS**}
2011	HOU	57	221	26	61	10	1	2	12	7	5	.276	.297	.357
2012	HOU	147	576	80	167	34	4	7	37	33	40	.290	.340	.399
2013	HOU	152	626	64	177	31	2	5	52	35	32	.283	.316	.363
2014	HOU	158	660	85	**225**	47	3	7	59	**56**	36	**.341**	.377	.453
2015	HOU	154	**638**	86	**200**	40	4	15	66	**38**	33	.313	.353	.459
2016	HOU	161	640	108	**216**	42	5	24	96	60	60	**.338**	.396	.531
Totals		829	3361	449	1046	204	19	60	322	199	206	.311	.354	.437

G = Games
AB = At-bats
R = Runs scored
H = Hits
2B = Doubles

3B = Triples
HR = Home runs
RBI = Runs batted in
SB = Stolen bases
BB = Bases on balls (walks)

BA = Batting average
OBP = On-base percentage
SLG = Slugging average
Bold = Led league

Major Honors
MLB All-Star Game: 2012, 2014–2016
AL Silver Slugger Award: 2014–2016
AL Gold Glove Award: 2015
MLB Player of the Year (chosen by MLB Players' Association): 2016

Chronology

May 6, 1990 José Altuve is born in Maracay, Venezuela.

March 6, 2007 Signs with the Houston Astros organization.

2007–2011 Bats .327 over five Minor League seasons.

July 20, 2011 Debuts in the Major Leagues with the Astros.

August 20, 2011 Belts an inside-the-park home run against San Francisco for his first Major League homer.

July 12, 2012 Plays in his first MLB All-Star Game.

July 13, 2013 Signs a four-year contract with the Astros.

September 16, 2014 Cracks his 211th hit of the season to break Craig Biggio's Astros record.

September 28, 2014 Strokes two hits in the season finale to win the AL batting title (.341) by .006.

July 14, 2015 Starts in an MLB All-Star Game for the first time.

October 8, 2015 Rips three hits in Game 1 of the AL Division Series versus Kansas City.

May 5, 2016 Hits a home run for a young cancer patient.

June 2016 Bats .420 in June to win the AL Player of the Month Award.

October 2, 2016 Wins the AL batting title (.338) by .020.

November 1, 2016 Becomes a father for the first time.

November 9, 2016 Named the Major Leagues' Player of the Year by the MLB Players' Association.

Glossary

batting average A statistic: hits divided by official at-bats (walks, hit-by-pitches, sacrifice flies, and sacrifice bunts don't count as official at-bats).

batting champion The player who has the highest batting average in the league.

Class-A One of four Minor League levels; from lowest to highest, they are Rookie Ball, Class-A, Double-A, and Triple-A.

cycle Achieved when a batter hits a single, double, triple, and home run in the same game.

engineer A person with scientific training who designs or builds complicated products, machines, systems, or structures.

epitome The perfect example.

fielding percentage A statistic: putouts plus assists divided by total chances.

five-tool Refers to a baseball player who can hit for a high average, hit for power, and run, throw, and field exceptionally well.

Goliath A giant who is featured in the Bible; he battled a boy named David and lost.

hit-and-run A designed play in which the base runner(s) run and then the batter swings.

Napoleon complex A condition in which a person tries to be extremely successful to overcome his or her shame at being short.

on-base percentage A statistic: hits plus walks plus hit-by-pitches divided by total plate appearances.

slugging average A statistic: total bases divided by official at-bats (a single is one total base, a double two, a triple three, and a home run four).

terminal cancer Cancer that cannot be cured and is expected to result in the death of the patient.

walk-off A plate appearance that results in a game-ending, winning run.

Further Reading

Books

Aretha, David. *Top 10 Hitters in Baseball.* New York, NY: Enslow Publishers, 2016.

Chandler, Matthew. *Side-By-Side Baseball Stars: Comparing Pro Baseball's Greatest Players.* North Mankato, MN: Capstone, 2015.

Jacobs, Greg. *The Everything Kids' Baseball Book: From Baseball's History to Today's Favorite Players—With Lots of Home Run Fun in Between!* Avon, MA: Adams Media, 2016.

Nagelhout, Ryan. *David Ortiz: World Series Champion.* New York, NY: Britannica Educational/Rosen, 2016.

Rauf, Don. *Miguel Cabrera: Triple Crown Winner.* New York, NY: Britannica Educational/Rosen, 2016.

Websites

Baseball Reference

baseball-reference.com

Search "José Altuve" to find career, season, and game stats on the Astros star.

ESPN

ESPN.com

Search "José Altuve" to find all the latest stories, stats, and videos on Altuve.

Houston Astros

houston.astros.mlb.com

This site includes team news, game coverage, Astros Fans Central, and bios of players—including José Altuve.

Index